A Prayer
for the
Children
of Zimbabwe

THE OUTREACH
FOUNDATION
OF THE PRESBYTERIAN CHURCH, INC.

Dear Friends in Christ,

No group is more oppressed than street children. This is a problem Presbyterians are facing.

There is good news for those children who call the streets home. Today, Presbyterian missionaries are working with street children in Zimbabwe, Kenya, and Brazil.

In Harare, Zimbabwe, Presbyterians have expanded their outreach ministry by starting a school at the downtown City Presbyterian Church. They have also created a relocation program at a farm nearby, where 128 children live. A resident facility, called the Lovemore House, provides a Christian home environment for twelve children. And, older boys and young men are learning new skills at Madzimbabwe Art Production.

Much work still needs to be done. Jesus made it clear how important the children of the world are. "Inasmuch as ye have done it unto one of the least of these my brethren, ye have done it unto me" (Matt. 25:40 KJV).

William T. Bryant
Executive Director

A Prayer for the Children of Zimbabwe

The Outreach Foundation
OF THE PRESBYTERIAN CHURCH, INC.

with Pam Kidd

PROVIDENCE HOUSE PUBLISHERS
Franklin, Tennessee

Printed in the United States of America

04   03   02   01   00   1   2   3   4   5

Library of Congress Catalog Card Number: 00-101250

ISBN: 1-57736-183-0

Cover design by Gary Bozeman

Cover photos and interior photos by Bill and Bette Bryant, Pam and David Kidd, and Nancy and Bill Warlick

PROVIDENCE HOUSE PUBLISHERS
238 Seaboard Lane • Franklin, Tennessee 37067
800-321-5692
www.providencehouse.com

PROLOGUE

The early morning light falls softly on the hard streets of downtown Harare. I breathe deeply. The smell of burning coal oil reminds me that even though it is midsummer back home in Tennessee, winter has arrived here in this little African country called Zimbabwe. I exhale. My breath freezes into a little cloud, then floats away.

I want to go home, I moan inwardly.

Before me a great gaggle of pathetic children gather along a low-slung rock wall that fronts the garden of a great stone church. A forbidding iron fence stands between the children and the church.

These are the street children of Zimbabwe, and I have traveled halfway around the world to write about them.

God, I don't want to be here, I continue my lament, as I silently recall the letter I had received from a Presbyterian missionary a few months back. "We have been praying that someone would come to Zimbabwe and meet our children, then tell the world about their terrible plight. God has told me you are the one," she had written.

At first I had tossed the letter on a stack of unanswered mail. At that moment I was knee-deep in our daughter's wedding and had no time for such faraway fantasies. But the letter gnawed at me—its words chased me from bridal luncheon and linen shower to celebratory dinner. Finally, one evening, I took an inventory of the loveliness of our life and gave in.

"God, You've made it perfectly clear. I'm mightily blessed, and I owe something back. Besides, Zimbabwe couldn't be all that bad."

Yet, beyond that seemingly faithful reaction to the missionary's call, more self-serving motives lurked. Now, in this grim setting, I had to be honest with myself. Part of the reason I had said "yes" to Zimbabwe was my desire to do something showy for God. I would write something pure and sweet, and back home the accolades would flow. People would look at me as if I were . . . one of God's chosen: Pam Kidd, heroine of the downtrodden!

So here I am, but instead of feeling heroic, I feel completely helpless. In the past days I had visited homeless children in stinking alleyways, where they sift through garbage bins for morsels of food. I

Forty thousand street CHILDREN die *each day* as a RESULT of malnutrition and PREVENTABLE *disease*

had sought them out in the backstreets, where they burrow at night in makeshift shelters of cardboard and rags.

It's only now, as I catch sight of a half-starved girl huddling with her baby brother in a single patch of sun, that my spirit breaks. Never have I felt such hopelessness—even the comfortable church that lies just beyond the crumbling sidewalk unapologetically shuns these children. *God*, I lash out, *I can't take any more of this. Why did You send me to this desolate place? Your children are hungry, God. They are ragged, cold, and barefoot—even Your so-called Christians reject them.*

Then I see the little beat-up car turning the corner. The girl's gaunt face brightens. "Mabhuwu," she calls, and others join in, "Mabhuwu is coming . . . Mabhuwu."

It is a name I have heard over and over as I have interviewed the street children. The woman called "Mabhuwu" is the reason I have come to this godforsaken spot as Sunday breaks over Harare's horizon. In interview after interview, the children have told me:

"Mabhuwu is the lady who gives tea and bread."

"Mabhuwu found me in the alley and took me to the doctor when I was sick."

"Mabhuwu's trying to help me find my grandmother."

"Mabhuwu gave me this blanket, which keeps me warm at night."

Gradually, I had wrapped all my hopes around this phantom woman of goodness. I imagined her, some rich, benevolent soul who had come to save these children out of the largess of her unending bounty. Her image kept me going as I struggled these last days with the terrible poverty of this economically and socially ravaged country, where one out of every four people is dying of AIDS.

Many stories of Mabhuwu filtered through the streets as I conducted my interviews: She had been a South African tennis star, a woman of prominence who had turned her attention toward the street children.

Now, I can't believe my eyes as a lone rattletrap car pulls up and a nondescript woman emerges. Her son helps her tug a huge aluminum pot of a dark, steaming liquid out of the trunk. With several loaves of sliced white bread tucked under their free arms, they turn toward the growing crowd of homeless children and adults who wait.

I stand in the shadow of an acacia tree that leans over the church's spiked fence. I shiver, realizing that this lone, obviously impoverished woman is the single star upon which these children hang their hope.

My God, why have you forsaken these babies? I see hunger, sickness, even death on their faces. God, how can this be? Where are Your angels? Where are You, God? Where are You!

I step out of the shadows and into a circle of sunlight to try to warm myself, and His answer comes. Clearly. Simply.

Here I am. You've been searching for Me all of your life. Now look into My face.

I raise my head and find myself toe-to-toe with the woman called Mabhuwu. Our eyes lock for a moment. She smiles, and the look on

Homeless children live in alleyways in Harare.

her face melts every doubt of God I have ever experienced.

As Mabhuwu turns back to the little children to fill their cups with warm tea and offer them fresh bread, groups of well-dressed Zimbabweans begin to arrive. They file past the children and straight through the iron gate, eyes set on the church ahead; not one acknowledges the scene that plays out before them.

Now, Mabhuwu shifts her attention to the sickest children. She begins dispensing spoons full of cough medicine. The children stand patiently in line, waiting, trusting, as baby birds trust.

I break away. I don't want the children to see me cry. They might mistake my tears for pity. It is the sheer beauty of the moment that causes me to weep.

I had answered God's call with small-minded, self-serving motives. God in His infinite patience called to show me something far greater than anything I could have imagined on my own. For all my life, I have longed for some epiphany—some chance to see an angel in human form.

A dirty stretch of street in Harare, Zimbabwe, has become my little spot of hallowed ground. Even better than an angel sighting, I have looked into the eyes of a poor, humble woman, and I have seen the eyes of God.

Street children graciously accept warm tea from the lady they call "Mabhuwu."

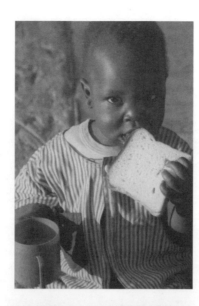

Brought by older brothers or sisters looking for work guarding cars, some street children are just toddlers.

To think, He sent *me* all the way to Africa so that I might look into His beautiful face. Then, He sent me safely home again so that I might tell all of you who will listen about Mabhuwu, the lady whom God has chosen to bring tea and bread to His children. That's how His kingdom comes, you know, through people no greater than you and me. As I tell you this, I can't help thinking that the mere telling of it is a privilege I do not deserve.

It took some urging to convince "the lady who brings tea and bread," to meet with my husband, David, and me. Finally she consented to visit with us at the home of a Presbyterian missionary couple in Harare who struggle to lend support to her unique ministry.

We had asked her to meet us for dinner at our hotel's restaurant. "How can I go to a restaurant," she had asked, "when children roam the streets begging for a bite to eat?"

Originally from the Northern Cape of Africa, the one the children call Mabhuwu was an avid tennis player who had risen to the ranks of a prestigious provincial tennis team. After her husband moved her and their three sons to Zimbabwe, her life began to shatter.

"I was always tennis mad. I married, had children, and continued to spend every spare minute on the tennis court. Sure, I went to church on Sundays. I thought I was a Christian, and I was quite content.

"Then my marriage broke down, and my husband found someone else. The Lord used disappointment, anger, and eventually unemployment to teach me the things I needed to learn. I found myself here in Harare, almost destitute, finally realizing that I needed God.

"In 1988, I went to a Christian meeting and the leader said, 'Everybody is worth something to God.'

"I thought, 'Could God really be interested in *me*?'

"Well, the leader had a call-up, and the Lord got my attention. I stepped forward and the joy was incredible. Back in my flat, I realized it was time to put my life in order. First I called my ex-husband and I said, 'Thank you . . . you gave me three sons . . . you brought me to Harare . . . I wouldn't have found God, if it weren't for you.'

"I went on to ask his forgiveness for the tennis, for not being home enough, and his forgiveness took away all my resentment.

"Next I made a list of all my wrongs. It went on for pages and pages. After I finished, I stood at the window and looked out into the night. 'Lord,' I said, 'if you can possibly forgive all this, send a star across the sky.' I know it's hard to believe, but at that moment, He sent a star shooting by my flat window, and I know I am forgiven. I take a match and set that book with all my wrongs aflame. I am free.

"I know that it's time to leave tennis, so I ask the Lord, 'What can I do for You?'

"He says, 'There's the street kids.'

"And I say, 'Smelly, runny nose street kids . . . not me, Lord.' And in the silence that follows, I give in and say, 'How should I start?'"

The *children* are BEAUTIFUL. They have *nothing* . . . but they can still SING

Today, Mabhuwu lives on the paltry income she receives as a part-time bookkeeper. She rises each morning by 4:00 A.M. to prepare tea and gather bread to serve the children who wait at the first light of day. Sometimes money for gas is a problem, and Mabhuwu walks to meet the children, carrying all she can. The rest of the day, she visits the children on the streets, solving their immediate problems and calling on the Presbyterian missionaries when needs beyond her resources arise.

"In Zimbabwe," Mabhuwu says, "poverty and AIDS are shameless. They take away the extended family. They send the children to live in the streets. And besides these, there are more hurdles and roadblocks and detours than you can imagine. People steal the children's blankets; the police lock them up; others have burned their squatter camps while they are out scavenging for food.

"Still, with the Lord's help, we can save these kids one by one. Past food and blankets, we need to give them lessons, help them get back in school, locate any living relatives, teach them to be self-supporting.

"At first I could afford to give the children vitamins, fruit, soap once a week . . . but money's tighter now. We live by prayer and we know joy.

"The children are beautiful. They have nothing . . . but they can still sing."

Pam Kidd
January 2000

9

Two little girls with reason to smile: After being rescued from the streets of Harare, they have found a home at Melfort Farm.

INTRODUCTION

Bad times have come to Zimbabwe. Poverty is rampant. Children are hungry, homeless, and orphaned. In this one south African country, as many as 600 thousand children have lost both their parents to AIDS. The network of extended families, once a mainstay of Zimbabwean culture, has been fragmented. Thousands of children find themselves without a home or caring family. Scenes of ragged children sleeping in alleys and eating from garbage bins are common. They are the street children of Zimbabwe.

When Reverend Bill and Nancy Warlick first walked down the streets of Harare, they were struck by the sheer numbers of homeless children. They found a direct relationship between the spread of the HIV/AIDS pandemic in Zimbabwe and the numbers of children living on the streets of Harare. In a country where AIDS was claiming one in every four adults, families were ripped apart and poverty was on the rise. The truth was simple: thousands of children had nowhere to go but to the streets.

Serving as missionaries for the Presbyterian Church in Zimbabwe, the Warlicks soon became deeply committed to the plight of the street children.

"How could we stand by and allow children to be treated as animals," Nancy Warlick asks, "to be left alone . . . out in the cold . . . to be hungry and uncared for?"

The Warlicks and several Zimbabwean Presbyterians initiated a once-a-week meal for street children at City Presbyterian Church in Harare. Soon children were flocking there for food, recreation, warm clothes, medical help, and even Bible study and prayer.

In answer to countless requests for a chance to go to school, the feeding program evolved into an informal school. Completely on their own, numbers of homeless children came in from the street to attend school each day.

Back in the United States, a Presbyterian elder—touched by the Warlicks' efforts, donated funds through the Outreach Foundation to purchase a house in Harare. "Lovemore" was established, a group home where boys could go to school and live in a family setting. Other

In Zimbabwe 600 *thousand* CHILDREN have been *orphaned* as the result of DEATH from AIDS-*related* diseases

donations helped establish Melfort Farm, a rural center where 128 former street children live, work, and attend school together. A third project, Madzimbabwe Art Production, was organized at the Kuwadzana Presbyterian Church, a few miles beyond Harare's city limits. Here, older boys have a chance to come in from the streets to study art and develop markets for their work.

Still, Lovemore's children need more clothes, school supplies, and money for school uniforms. At Melfort Farm, few children have shoes, warm clothes for the winter, or adequate school supplies. Madzimbabwe Art Production lacks proper teaching tools, money for instructors, and room for new students.

And, back in the streets of Zimbabwe, children are still eating from garbage cans, sleeping under cardboard, begging for pennies. On cold nights, they dream of having a decent meal, a blanket, and a chance to go to school.

A PRAYER FOR THE CHILDREN OF ZIMBABWE reveals the work the Warlicks are doing on behalf of the Presbyterian Church (U.S.A.) in partnership with the Outreach Foundation and Presbyterians in Zimbabwe. The book details the ministries of the Presbyterian Church in Zimbabwe—their histories, current state, and projected futures—and introduces the children whose outlooks have become more hopeful. As Presbyterians pray for each individual child, many of the children pray daily for ". . . the Presbyterians who changed our lives."

Through the Warlicks' dedication, the words "Presbyterian" and "hope" are becoming more and more synonymous for growing numbers of street children.

12

The Ministries

Lovemore House gives former STREET *children* a Christian HOME environment and is LOCATED in a *suburb* outside of HARARE. *Twelve* boys currently LIVE at *Lovemore*

GILBERT CHIKUNI,
an effervescent young man
who shines with Christian
love, has served as Love-
more House's director since
1998. Along with his wife,
Senzeni, and infant son,
Tinashe, he lives perma-
nently with the boys of
Lovemore. He worked
hand-in-hand with Maury
Mendenhall, a Presbyterian
Church (U.S.A.) mission
volunteer, to get the home
opened. They have been a
team ever since.

"We are a family," Gilbert
says about the group at
Lovemore, "living together,
helping each other grow. It's
wonderful to be the director
here, to be part of a team
who brings hope to the
people of Zimbabwe.

"Without the Presbyterian
Church, I ask myself, where
would these boys be but
back on the street? Your
prayers encourage us. Keep
praying for us. We are
praying for you."

LOVEMORE HOUSE

The big stucco house sits back from the street surrounded by an expansive walled-in yard. Gardens running along the wall are thick with rape—a plant that is chopped and cooked into a traditional African dish similar to kale or collards. Vines curl about long, well-tended rows of potato mounds. A tire swing hangs on a rope from an acacia tree, and the sound of children's laughter livens the air.

Named for the street on which it sits, Lovemore House seems light years away from nearby Harare, a teeming city where scores of street children sleep in alleys and scavenge through garbage for something—anything—to eat. Lovemore is, in fact, a sanctuary from the terrible street life once endured by its residents.

Maury Mendenhall, a Presbyterian Church (U.S.A.) mission volunteer, worked with director Gilbert Chikuni to bring five boys from the streets of Harare into the home. The group home welcomed its first residents in April of 1998; now, twelve boys live at Lovemore.

Located in a suburb of Harare called Cranborne, Lovemore provides a Christian, family-style living environment for children who have a strong desire to leave life on the streets behind. Lovemore enables its residents to go to school and in appropriate cases helps each boy re-establish ties with his family.

Inside, Linah, a gentle-hearted Zimbabwean woman, oversees Lovemore's kitchen—smiling a sweet smile as she stirs a huge pot of sadza, similar to grits and the staple of African cuisine. Two boys sit nearby at the kitchen table, reading their schoolbooks and savoring the warmth and, yes, the safety of Linah's kitchen.

In the sitting room, two more boys sit laughing and talking with Gilbert. At first glance, Gilbert might be a big brother, or even better, a father, to these boys rather than a mere house parent. Back in the first bedroom, a younger boy folds clean clothes and places them in a drawer. Before joining Gilbert in the sitting room, he stops and lovingly smooths the blanket that covers his bed.

MADZIMBABWE ART PRODUCTION

Moving away form the bustle of Harare, the road leading to the Kuwadzana Presbyterian Church grows narrow and dusty. A woman, as majestic as a queen, walks down a side lane balancing a huge basket of greens atop her head. Ahead, another woman artfully stacks vivid red tomatoes at an open-air produce stand. A baby is secured to her back by a colorful blue and gold shawl.

There is no grass surrounding the small, low-slung concrete and mud houses you pass along the way. Here and there, women sweep dirt

Madzimbabwe Art Production gives older boys and young men from the street a place to live and study art.

yards with brooms fashioned from straw and twigs. The landscape appears stark until we swing through the gates of the church where Madzimbabwe Art Production is headquartered.

Inside the walls that surround the church grounds, the dust gives way to a stretch of green grass. Entering the courtyard is like stepping onto a sort of emerald isle in the midst of Africa's poverty. Birds sing in the garden, roses bloom, and trees bud with pink and red blossoms. There is a slight, pleasant smell of burning coal in the cool air. The morning sunlight falls over a girl in a yellow dress as she bends over a basin washing teacups. Her name is Patience. The daughter of the pastor, she works in the church office answering the phone and studying in her spare time for her high school diploma.

The minister of the church, a radiant middle-aged man aptly named Jonah, greets us in his simple office, eager to talk of the art school that is based here. He is delighted that the Presbyterians have lent their support to this project, designed to give older boys from the street a place to come and study art.

*Melfort Farm children
build a basketball
court.*

"The young people on the streets . . . they could be teachers, doctors, or artists if only someone is able to help them," he says, eyes shining. "I see these boys come from the streets to learn the art, and I think, 'They will become good men.' It will never come out of my memory that there are people everywhere who love Jesus and want to do good in His name. They are the ones who have made this project possible. I wish I could thank them all."

MELFORT FARM

Melfort Farm provides a permanent home for 128 former street children, and its beginnings can be traced to the efforts of Bill and Nancy Warlick to establish a ministry for the street children of Harare. In 1995, along with organizations and other community leaders, the

Warlicks organized the Presbyterian feeding program, where the children could come in off the streets for food and clothing. As the needs of the street children became more pronounced, the school was started. Finally, with the help of local agencies, thirty-one children moved from the streets to a farm twenty-five miles outside of Harare that once served as a government training center. Now Melfort Farm, the facilities include bare-bones dormitories, a dining hall, and a nearby primary school. A secondary school is a few miles away.

In the children's rooms, neatly made beds line the walls. They store their few possessions in cardboard boxes. There is no heat in the winter except in the kitchen, where stoves are fired by a wood-burning furnace. There are no chairs and tables in the dining hall. Most of the children lack shoes. Their clothes are second-hand and often tattered. They play soccer with balls hand-fashioned from rags and twine, and playground equipment is primarily old tires and trees. A group of musically inclined children have formed a band making their own drums and marimbas and shakers. At night, groups of children gather to sing and dance, enjoying the band's music.

There are only a few ragged books in the library, and the charts and learning tools at the school are all hand-lettered. There are no maps,

Children at Melfort Farm say they are very happy to have their own beds.

Melfort Farm children have made their own drums, marimbas, and shakers.

The facilities at Melfort Farm are minimal, yet the children are so happy to be off the streets.

"Do YOU love Me?" Jesus asks, "then, FEED my *sheep"*

globes, or teaching models, no computers or calculators, no science labs, no physical education equipment.

Recent visitors to the rural school found the children busy making bricks and digging foundations with simple handmade tools. An American foundation called Hoops for Hope had recently donated two basketball hoops to Melfort, and the children were enthusiastically building their own basketball court completely from "scratch."

The children are happy, even thrilled to have their own beds, their own blankets, enough food, and a chance to go to school. When art supplies are available, some draw pictures of blooming flowers and shining stars for their walls.

Ask the boys and girls how they feel about Melfort Farm, and they become animated—they smile, they laugh, they talk about warm blankets and good food. They say how "good" the Presbyterians in America are—more than one mentions the word "heaven."

The
Children

When you LIVE in the *street,* you *don't* have a bed or a BLANKET, and you are *hungry* and AFRAID

DEAR GOD, HEAR CHAMUNORWA

Age 14, Lovemore House

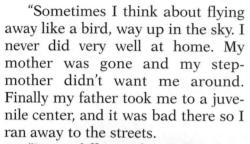

"Sometimes I think about flying away like a bird, way up in the sky. I never did very well at home. My mother was gone and my stepmother didn't want me around. Finally my father took me to a juvenile center, and it was bad there so I ran away to the streets.

"It was different than I thought it would be on the streets. I thought there would be a freedom there, but I discovered that I wouldn't have enough food and not even a blanket.

"Life on the streets was never a good thing, and all I thought about was how I would never be able to go to school again . . . how I would never be able to grow up and be a pilot like I wanted.

"When I went to the Presbyterian church for food, they told me I could come to school there; so I left the streets every morning and went to school. I think it was God who helped bring me to Lovemore.

"I think I might be able to be a pilot now. Someday I will fly up in the clouds and around lakes checking on fishing boats . . . but I will always be thinking of the children left on the streets. I will be praying that they will have a chance for a good life, too."

CHAMUNORWA suffered under his stepmother's care. Before he left his home village for the streets of Harare, neighbors described him as delinquent, going without proper food and missing school. The Lovemore staff sees him as a boy eager to make a success of his life. He is striving to do well in school so that he might fulfill his dream of being a pilot.

DEAR GOD, HEAR AARON

Age 14, Lovemore House

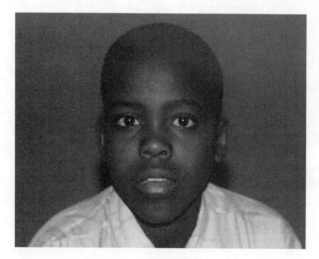

"When you live in the street, you don't have a bed or a blanket, and you are hungry and afraid. You might think someone is a good person and they tell you they will give you a biscuit if you get in their car. Then they do bad things to you, and they never give you a biscuit.

"The streets are the worst place in the world. I think Lovemore is the best place. People care about me here. I have a bed here. We have a dog and a fence and burglar bars on the windows. Lovemore is my safe place. When I go to my bed at night, I pray and ask God to let all the other children in the streets find a safe place, too."

DEAR GOD, HEAR JUSTICE
Age 16, Melfort Farm

"When I was six, I ran away to the streets of Harare. I learned to eat from garbage bins and to sleep on the verandas of shops. I guarded

cars for money and sometimes begged. I started sniffing glue with some of the older boys because it made me feel not afraid. When you're high, you don't think of the bad things.

"I was filled with joy when the Presbyterians told me I was important to God. Then they invited me to come and stay at the farm. To sleep inside a room, to have a bed, a blanket, and a chance to go to school is the best thing that has ever happened to me.

"When I advanced to the secondary school, I had to get up very early before the first light to get there on time. The walk was many kilometers. When the Presbyterians heard about the distance I walked each day, they brought me a bicycle, and now I don't have to leave for school until 6:00 A.M.

AARON
made his way to the streets of Harare from a small village where a mean-spirited stepmother had made his life unbearable. The stepmother favored her own sons and actually withheld food and shelter from Aaron. He left home at age twelve, sleeping first in a market, then in a bus terminal, and finally in the back alleys. Aaron was treated kindly by the workers at the Presbyterian feeding program, and he eventually started attending school there on his own. Then he was recommended to the staff of Lovemore House and was one of the first boys to be taken into the home.

Described as a "bright child with a brilliant sense of humor," Aaron seems to have a good future ahead. He says he would like to become an engineer " . . . to make cars . . . that's something that will help people in the long distance."

"Now what I want most is to finish school. I want to continue all the way up to the university. I want to be a scientist. I want to find out things by myself . . . without anyone telling me."

DEAR GOD, HEAR NYEMBESI
Age 15, Melfort Farm

"First my mother died. Then my father died too. So, one day, I left my home village with friends, and we made our way to Harare. The first night I slept under a tree in a park, and I felt afraid, but I didn't have any other place to go. Some of the other kids showed me how to eat from the garbage bins, and sometimes that food would make me sick. I started begging for food outside the hotels, and then I heard about the Presbyterians. I went to the church for food, and they asked about my history. When I told them all that had happened to me, they contacted the farm and asked if I could come and go to school.

"I had been sleeping in the cold, without a blanket, covering up with cardboard boxes. Here, I have been given good food, a bed, and my own blanket . . . all for free. And I can go to school every day.

"God is so good to me. Maybe He will even help me become an airline hostess. Then I will fly to many places and have a beautiful home, and someday I will come back to Melfort Farm and do kind things for the children here."

DEAR GOD, HEAR RODGERS
Age 17, Melfort Farm

"The worst thing about being on the streets is, if you grow up there, you will get old without ever going to school. That's a big problem.

"I was seven when I first came to the streets. My mother had gone away, and my father had lost his job in a factory sewing cloth. For a time we sold firewood, then I worked herding sheep and tending gardens. Then my father remarried, and my stepmother said bad things about me and caused my father to beat me. I wasn't welcome anywhere, so I came to the streets.

"In the streets, I met with many problems. I spent whole days without eating. I survived by looking after cars and asking people for food. Sometimes when I got money, I would buy glue for sniffing and beer. When I was drunk, other boys would come and steal from me and beat me up.

"I was told that if I visited the Presbyterians, they would give me food. They were nice to me and tried to help me solve my problems. They invited me to a church service and to school. I visited the Presbyterian Bible studies, and I heard about Jesus. My life was changed. When they asked me to come to the farm, I thought first about the school and then about the bed. The first night having a bed of my own and a blanket, I thought I was in heaven.

"Now I want to become a pastor. I want to finish school here, find a boarding school, and then go to the university. I think someday I can help others . . . like the Presbyterians have helped me."

TONDERAI
has become a model member of the Lovemore family. He is responsible and smart and has emerged as a leader who influences the other boys to do their best in home chores and at school.

"When I grow up," he says, "I want to be a policeman so I can take care of people and help keep them safe."

DEAR GOD, HEAR TONDERAI
Age 13, Lovemore House

"I had gone to the streets when I was twelve. There wasn't enough food for my family after my father died, and I thought I could earn money guarding cars. But I found it difficult to get money, the police harassed me, and often I had to beg for food.

"There is a lady who comes to the streets to give tea and bread to the children. She told me I could go to the Presbyterian church and go to school. I was happy to hear that and so I went there. Next, the Presbyterians told me there was this place for boys who wanted to go to school. It was called Lovemore. They chose me to go.

MUZONDIWA, in spite of every imaginable obstacle, lives in hope. As a talented athlete, he plays on one of Zimbabwe's leading soccer teams and has every chance of becoming a professional player. The Lovemore staff sees him as one of their most appreciative family members and reports that he works very hard in school and stays focused on doing well, often volunteering for extra work and striving to be a good role model for the other boys.

"Without Lovemore," says Gilbert Chikuni, the home director, "all of Muzondiwa's talents would have gone down the drain. He has a good future now."

"I came here to Lovemore and they said . . . 'This is the bed where you will sleep,' and 'This is the trunk where you can put your clothes,' and 'This is where you will come to eat' . . . and I felt, oh, very happy.

"I wish I could tell all children: 'Don't go to the streets. It's cold . . . you won't have a place to sleep . . . you will have to eat from garbage bins . . . you might be killed . . . this is what happens on the streets.' I wish I could change the world so no one would have to beg for food and children wouldn't be abused and people could love each other and there could be freedom for everyone."

DEAR GOD, HEAR MUZONDIWA
Age 14, Lovemore House

"My life was never very good. Even my name 'Muzondiwa' means 'unwanted child.' When I was two weeks old, my mother dumped me in a stack of old tires. The police picked me up and took me to my grandmother, and when she gave me back to my mother, she dumped me again . . . this time wrapping me in rags and leaving me in a beer hall.

"No one ever really wanted me except my grandmother and she was too poor to buy enough food or pay my school fees.

"After I ended up on the streets, some people at the church told me about Lovemore, and they asked me to come here. I'm going to finish school and become a soccer player, and later maybe I'll have a job in a bank.

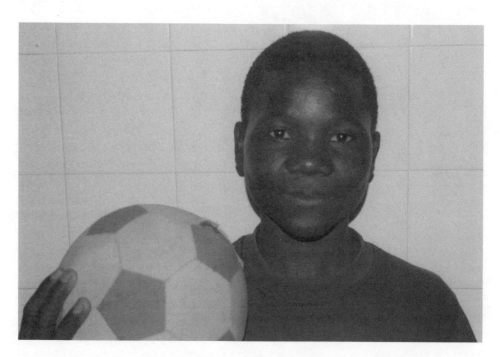

"Inside my head I ask God to help me reach my goals, to help me in school and with soccer, and especially to help me forgive others and not join in conflict. Someday, I think God will give me another name: 'Amon.' It will mean 'someone good.'"

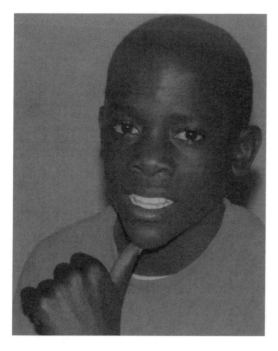

DEAR GOD, HEAR JOHN

Age 16, Lovemore House

"Kids don't run away from home for nothin'. Some kids' parents die. Other kids don't have good parents and they're poor and they get hungry and get into bad trouble for stealing.

"But the children on the streets aren't living a good life either. If you get some money, bigger, meaner boys might take it from you. There are men who come to the streets to try to do not-good things to you. There's never enough food, and sometimes you get so hungry you eat unprotected food, and you can die from that.

"What a difference Lovemore has made for me. At night when I go to bed, it is good to have a place to sleep with a blanket . . . and you can even have two if you want. We have enough food here, and the best thing is . . . I go to school. When I grow up, I am going to be a pastor and have a place like Lovemore where children can come and have good food and clothes and an education . . . and love."

JOHN
is a boy who will achieve his ambitions. Never knowing his father and abandoned by his mother as an infant, John lived with various relatives before finding himself homeless on the streets of Harare.

John lived a rough life stealing and fighting for survival. He eventually made his way to the Presbyterian feeding program, where he came face to face with God's love. Today, as a follower of Christ, John studies diligently with the goal of becoming a pastor.

"Every day," he says, "I pray for all the Presbyterians in America who have helped me find my way."

DEAR GOD, HEAR RACHEAL

Age 16, Melfort Farm

"I left home when I was twelve along with my brother and some friends. We had no father, and my mother had no money for food and school fees, so we thought we could earn money in Harare and go to school there.

"I was afraid when I saw how the other children were living, eating food from garbage bins and sleeping in front of buildings. My brother

HAMZA
was nine years old when, fearing for his life, he fled from an abusive home. Born into an atmosphere of rejection, he was abandoned by his mother and was frequently abused by his father. Passed from one relative to the next, Hamza found peace for a while with his maternal grandmother. His grandmother's death devastated Hamza, and when he was returned to his father, he was beaten unmercifully. That's when Hamza took to the streets full time.

Rescued by the Lovemore staff, Hamza lives with hope for the first time in his life. Although he requires encouragement, an occasional "Good, Hamza!" from the Lovemore staff helps move him through his difficulties. Currently, he is showing great improvement in school and says he wants to work in a home like Lovemore when he grows up "so I can help other children as I have been helped."

was just seven, and it was tough to get food for both of us.

"One day I was walking in the street and a lady from the Presbyterian church came and said, 'Come and we will give you food.' I took my brother's hand and went with her to the church and found that they offered lessons there, too. From then on, I kept going to school from the street until they asked me if I would like to come to the farm. I said, 'Yes, if my brother can come, too.'

"We are kept very well here. We are able to eat well-prepared food, and we can go to school and have a safe place to sleep. My vision is to complete my education at the farm and then to study how to look after other kids in the streets. I am longing to help other children, and I pray that this can happen."

DEAR GOD, HEAR HAMZA
Age 11, Lovemore House

"People aren't happy to see children on the streets. They say 'Go back home!' But what they don't know is what happens at home . . . they don't know that a lot of kids can never go back home again.

"On the streets, you have nowhere to sleep if it rains, the drains fill up with water and the police chase you away from the doorways. You get cold.

"To me, Lovemore is the best place in the world. I have good food to eat and . . . to have my own bed . . . that makes me very happy."

JOHN MOYO

DEAR GOD, HEAR JOHN MOYO
Age 22,
Madzimbabwe Art Production

"If I had to think of a single word to describe life on the streets, the word would be 'lonely.' I think of the cold nights, the rainy season, the days when I couldn't get anything to eat. One day a friend told me the City Presbyterian Church was offering free meals for kids from the streets. I went hoping for food. Then a lady at the church said, 'John, would you like to do art with us?' and my life began to change. Always it was in my heart to create something good, and when I do art, I am happy. I hope someday to live like everyone else . . . to improve my skills, to study painting on canvas . . . and then to teach other people as the church has taught me."

was eight years old when the complexities of a broken family, the deprivation of profound poverty, and the terror of civil war in his childhood home in Mozambique drove him to the streets of Harare.

He remained a child of the streets until he joined the Presbyterian Church's Madzimbabwe Art Production at age eighteen. This particular project targets older street children, offering them a chance to use innate artistic skills to move from homelessness to self-sufficiency.

Currently, John rents a tiny room in a small concrete house near Kuwadzana Church. In the open courtyard, he joins other young men who work with metal, woodcuts, and batik.

In 1998, John was baptized at Kuwadzana Church, surrounded by a joyous congregation and the several Presbyterian volunteers who work at the Madzimbabwe project. John supports himself through the sale of his original batiks and greeting cards. He has displayed a keen interest in studying additional art forms, and instructors at Madzimbabwe express high expectations for John's artistic potential.

DEAR GOD, HEAR TARISAI
Age 16, Melfort Farm

"I was fourteen when my older brother talked me into going to the streets. My brother is blind, and he needed me to lead him through the streets and help him earn money by begging. We came to Harare by bus from my village far away.

"Soon we were not having anything to eat, not taking a bath or washing our clothes. When it rained, we tried to find shelter in doorways. Some of the street kids were sniffing glue and drinking, and I was trying not to do that.

"It was the Presbyterian church that offered me food and some clean clothes. Then they asked if I would like to come to school there at the church in the mornings. So I left my brother to beg in the streets with his friends, and I started to school.

"When I was invited to the farm, I knew it was going to be a good place. Here I have a good place to sleep, a place to wash my clothes. I can go to church and sing, and I have a chance to finish my education.

"I wonder about the people who have helped us—the Presbyterians in the U.S.A. I think about them and say prayers for them. They have given me everything good that I have."

DEAR GOD, HEAR SHINGIRAI
Age 9, Lovemore House

At least 40 PERCENT of the *street* CHILDREN of Harare are *infected* with HIV

"There's nothing good about living on the street. People scold you, and policemen can hit you if they want, and sometimes when you eat from garbage bins you get terribly sick and there's no one to care. You could die on the streets and who would know?

"I think I'm going to have a good future now . . . because I go to school and because I'm trying to listen to what God tells me to do.

"When I pray, I ask God to give all the street children a safe place like Lovemore House."

DEAR GOD, HEAR TICHAONA
Age 15, Melfort Farm

"I don't know what happened to my mother, but I ended up with my father and stepmother. My stepmother told many lies. She gave food to her own children and would give me no food. One day I missed school because I was very hungry and needed to find food. When I came home, my father beat me. That's when I decided I had to leave.

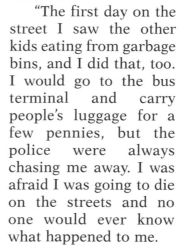

"The first day on the street I saw the other kids eating from garbage bins, and I did that, too. I would go to the bus terminal and carry people's luggage for a few pennies, but the police were always chasing me away. I was afraid I was going to die on the streets and no one would ever know what happened to me.

"One day a lady who came to the streets offering us tea and bread said, 'Please come to visit the Presbyterian church; they will give you food.' I went only for food, but the Presbyterians made me believe I could have a better life. They told me I was loved by God. They invited me to school, and then they told me about the farm.

"What I liked first when I arrived was the nice food and then I went to school and I liked that, too. Now I think of being a mechanic because, I think, where there are broken cars, there's money. I will have a home someday. I will have a bright future. Now when the days turn cold and rainy, I remember the street . . . how it was there . . . and I feel happy and very blessed."

SHINGIRAI had been abandoned by his mother and was living on the streets of Harare by age seven. He became a resident of Lovemore House at age nine and was quickly enfolded as a responsible, enthusiastic member of the Lovemore family. He loves to work in the garden, growing potatoes and greens for mealtime. Although he had never been to school until he came to Lovemore, reports of his progress are favorable.

DEAR GOD,
HEAR EMMANUEL
Age 9, Lovemore House

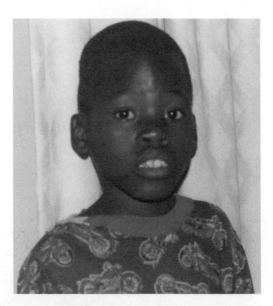

EMMANUEL, whose father died before he was born and whose mother abandoned him, was left to beg on the streets of Harare with his blind grandmother. As he grew older, he gradually lost touch with what family he had and took to the streets full time.

Because he wanted to learn to read and write, he began attending the school for street children at the City Presbyterian Church. Teachers at the informal school recognized Emmanuel's potential and, when a Presbyterian elder funded Lovemore House, a place was made for Emmanuel within the group family home.

Today, Emmanuel is one of the best students in his class and is striving for order in his life. The Lovemore staff has located Emmanuel's mother and is encouraging him to re-establish a relationship with her. The staff is searching for a way to enable her to start a small business selling vegetables so she might recover her self-esteem and move toward reclaiming her family.

The odds are that two of these Zimbabwean children will lose both of their parents and live on the streets.

"There are many dangers on the street. Some kids get beat up or hit by cars. Some end up sniffing glue . . . and that can make you lose your mind.

"If the streets are the worst place in the world, then Lovemore is the best. People care about each other here . . . like a family."

ACTION SUGGESTIONS

The 209th General Assembly of the Presbyterian Church (U.S.A.) designated July 1, 2000, to June 15, 2001, as the Year of the Child. What a wonderful opportunity we have to become personally involved as a church.

1. Circulate the stories in A Prayer for the Children of Zimbabwe with the staff, session, and mission committees of your congregation. Request that they prayerfully seek ways to acquaint the entire congregation with the plight of the street children worldwide.

2. Use the stories from the book as "Minutes for Mission."

3. Request copies to be used with the Women of the Church, youth groups, and church school classes. Encourage the whole congregation to engage in prayer for these little ones wherever they may be in the world. Pray for insight into how we as Presbyterians can help to alleviate the problem.

4. Contact the Outreach Foundation of the Presbyterian Church or Worldwide Ministries Division of the Presbyterian Church (U.S.A.) for more information and for resources that are available.

Right now, around the WORLD, an estimated ONE MILLION *children* are living on the STREETS

THE OUTREACH FOUNDATION

The Outreach Foundation is a Validated Missions Support Group of the Presbyterian Church (U.S.A.). For more than twenty years, the Outreach Foundation has enabled Presbyterians to:

- send out more evangelistic missionaries
- organize new congregations at home and abroad
- assist partner churches in evangelism, church construction, and leadership development
- participate in short-term mission trips and work camps

Our mission is to renew a passion for Christ-centered holistic evangelism and mission in and through the Presbyterian Church (U.S.A.).

The foundation accepts tax-exempt donations, which will fund its work. Additional opportunities to share the love of God with the street children of Zimbabwe abound. Five dollars will buy a child a year's school supplies; ten dollars will buy a blanket; fourteen dollars will buy a pair of shoes. Donations to the Outreach Foundation go directly to the field designated.

Contact the Outreach Foundation via telephone at 800-791-5023, visit the website at www.outreachfoundation.com, or write to the foundation at the following address:

The Outreach Foundation
318 Seaboard Lane, Suite 205
Franklin, Tennessee 37067

Approximately *half* of ALL the *world's* HIV/AIDS cases are in *Africa*. Zimbabwe is the hardest HIT *country* on the African continent